Presented to

_____

By

_____

REMEMBER
THE
PROMISE

REMEMBER
THE
PROMISE

ALVIN N. ROGNESS

AUGSBURG Publishing House
Minneapolis, Minnesota

REMEMBER THE PROMISE

Copyright © 1978 Augsburg Publishing House

Library of Congress Catalog Card No. 76-27082

International Standard Book No. 0-8066-1619-9

Design: David Koechel

Photos: David Koechel, pages 8, 16, 28, 38, 44, 54, 74; Wayne Allison, 20; Dale Beers, 32; Camerique, 58; Keith Heermann, 66; Wallowitch, 79.

Scripture quotations unless otherwise noted are from the Revised Standard Version of the Bible, copyright 1946, 1952, and 1971 by the Division of Christian Education of the National Council of Churches.

Manufactured in the United States of America

"And we desire each one of you to show
the same earnestness in realizing
the full assurance of hope until the end,
so that you may not be sluggish,
but imitators of those who through faith
and patience inherit the promises."

Hebrews 6:11-12

HOW PROMISING BEGAN

It's no fun to make promises, and sometimes it's no fun at all to keep them. Who started this business of promises anyway?

It all started with God. He made promises to Adam and Eve, and he's been at it ever since. He made promises to Noah and to Abraham and to Moses. He has made promises to you and to me.

And God keeps his promises. He never goes back on them. He doesn't even say, "You have to do this or that before I keep my promise." He makes the promise, and he keeps it. It's as simple as that.

But you can make it hard for him to give you what he promises. He promises to help you get rid of sin, but if you aren't interested, he won't twist your arm and make you.

That's the kind of God he is. He loves you and respects you so much that he won't sit you down and make you take what he wants to give you. He waits for you to say, "OK, give me what you promised."

Long before you knew about it, you were ushered into this world of God's promises. Your parents did it for you in Baptism. They knew about all the wonderful promises God makes for us in Baptism, and they said, "That's what we want for our child." So they brought you to church, and you were baptized in the name of the Father and the Son and the Holy Spirit. God invited you to live with him, and because you were too small to say yes, your parents said yes for you.

Later, as you grew, you began to understand. In Sunday school and church services you learned, and you joined others in confessing your faith and saying yes. Then in confirmation you said the kind of yes that your parents said at your Baptism.

Now you are in the thick of the world of promises. You could still back out. You could say you want nothing to do with God. But God wants to capture you with his promises and make life different for you. Wouldn't it be too bad if you backed out on that?

THE BIG PROMISE

God promises to give you himself. In that one promise he becomes your Father, your Savior, your Friend, your Lord. And you become his child.

Maybe it's something like when parents adopt a child. They sign a document promising to have this child be *their* child. They don't say specifically that they will feed the child, change his diapers, care for him when he's sick, send him to school, guide him to do right, or correct him when he does wrong. But that's what they mean when they make the one big promise. A hundred little promises are included in the one big one.

The Bible tells how God adopted Abraham and his family. God didn't love other families less than Abraham's, but God had a special job for Abraham's family. Through this family God promised to send a Savior for the whole world. This special promise was called a *covenant*.

After Jesus came, God made a new covenant. This new covenant included all the families of the earth—everyone!—because Jesus died for all of us.

In Baptism God makes this new covenant with you. He promises to give you himself. And with that one big promise, he assures you of all you need for this life, and of life with him in heaven forever.

Couldn't we have the small promises without the big one? Couldn't God give us food and health and pleasure without giving us himself? It may not be comfortable to have him around all the time.

The point is he wants *you* for himself. Why do you think he makes a covenant with you? He loves you, that's why. He wants to be your Father. He doesn't just want to send you gifts through the mail, as if you are a stranger. He wants you in his family.

That's why he gives you himself.

WHAT YOU HAVE PROMISED

It's not only God who makes one big promise. As a Christian, you do too. God promises you himself, and you promise him yourself.

If you enlist in the army during a war, you promise to be loyal to your country, to fight the enemy, to trust your leader, and to obey his commands.

You and God are in this business of promises together. He recruits you, and you enlist. You make promises to each other. That's what a *covenant* means.

As a child of God, a Christian, you make many smaller promises. You agree to listen to him, to follow him, to renounce all evil, to trust him, and to keep learning from him.

In the baptismal and confirmation services, you "renounce the devil, and all his works, and all his ways." You also confess your faith in the Triune God and promise to continue steadfast in this faith to the end.

You might say, "That's more than I bargained for." But as a Christian, can you settle for less? Can you be against evil half the time? Can you follow Christ only when you feel like it? If you want this half-way stuff, you might as well not promise at all. Being a Christian is a full-time business.

It's really not any fun on a part-time basis. The fun—and the glory—come when you say, "God, give me everything you have promised. I'm willing. Take me with you the whole way."

WHAT GOD DOES NOT PROMISE

You may be handsome or beautiful, and you may not be. Physical beauty is only skin deep. God has not promised to make you a Hollywood model.

You may have a high IQ, and you may not. Intelligence that can be measured by tests is only one kind of ability. You may have many other kinds. God does not promise you will be a genius.

You may be a good athlete, or you may be clumsy. God doesn't much care, so he makes no promises. Use the abilities you have, and don't wish for others.

You may get rich, but God doesn't promise that either. Much money may even destroy you, and God doesn't want you destroyed.

You may have many friends, or few. God cares more that you be a friend than that you collect friends.

You may live a long life, or you may die at 20. God may want you to have a long life,

but he's more concerned that you have a good life.

You may get a good job, or you may have to settle for work you'd rather not do. God has his own employment office, and you can work for him in any kind of job.

You may have eyes to see with and ears to hear with. Many people are blind or deaf. God doesn't necessarily promise to heal them. But he has ways to fill their lives with good things anyway.

"But," you say, "doesn't God want most of these things for us?" Yes, probably. But he knows that even if he gave them all to you, every one, your life might not be either happy or good.

He has something better for you. He promises that if you let him give you the kingdom of God and his righteousness, then everything else you need will come to you.

And this kingdom can be yours, with no strings attached. It can be yours right now, and also forever.

PROMISE YOURSELF

You touch a live wire and get burned, or you smoke and get sick, and you say, "I'll never do that again." You make a promise to yourself.

Such promises may not seem as important as promises made to your mother or to the doctor. Who will know if you break a promise to yourself?

You will know, of course. And you are as important as the doctor or your mother, even more important *to you.* Break a promise to yourself, and you disappoint yourself. Keep it up, and you become one big disappointment—to yourself. Your self-respect zooms down to zero.

In his play *Hamlet,* Shakespeare says, "To thine own self be true, and it must follow, as the night the day, thou can'st not then be false to any man."

Except for the promises you make to God, the most important ones you'll ever make are those you make to yourself.

You will fail sometimes. In a weak or stupid moment, you may break a promise. But the very worst thing you could do would be to say, "Well, I'll probably break it, so I won't make any promise to myself ever." Then you give up on yourself.

That would really disappoint God. He can put up with your trying and failing. Remember, one of his great promises is to forgive you when you fail, and to help you in the next try.

Have you heard of the word *integrity?* You can count on people who have integrity. When they make promises, they try to keep them. If they fail, they don't try to weasel out of it by lying or dredging up excuses. They're honest with themselves and with others. And people honor them even when they fail.

You are very important to you. Don't sell yourself short by never making promises to yourself. And don't disappoint yourself and lose your integrity by breaking those promises.

HE LETS
YOU DISOBEY

There were two brothers in the family. The younger asked his father for half the property, so he could leave the country and be on his own. The father didn't like it, but he let him go. The son made a mess of his life, and he knew it. Then he came home.

Remember, the Lord told this story. We call it the prodigal son story, but it's really a story about the father. And the father is God.

You see, the remarkable thing about God is that he lets you do what he doesn't want you to do. He gives you freedom to disobey him. He gives you freedom to mess up your life.

You might ask, "Why doesn't he lock up his children when they want to do what's wrong?" You wouldn't really like that, would you? Then it would be as if God were running a prison or a zoo. He is the Father of a family, and he wants his children to do the right thing because they want to, not because they have to.

When the son came home and said, "I have sinned against you," did the father turn him out? Did he say, "You sure have. If you're really sorry, OK, but you'll have to show me you've changed. Take a job in the next town for a year and prove you've come to your senses. Then you can come home."

You know the story. The father didn't say that. He threw a big party for his son. He was overjoyed that his son was back home—no questions asked.

That's the way God is. He'll be terribly hurt if you leave him and disobey him. But he has promised he will never cast out those who come to him.

Your dad may say, "No, you can't have the car. You have to stay home tonight." And he may be right. He's only trying to protect you, because he loves you.

But God takes longer risks than your dad. God lets you go your own way. He doesn't like to see you make mistakes. But he wants you to be with him, not because you *have* to, but because you *want* to.

THE COMMAND AND THE PROMISE

Only one of the Ten Commandments—the Fourth—has a specific promise attached: "Honor your father and your mother . . . that it may go well with you" (Deut. 5:16).

God singles out your behavior toward your parents for three reasons: he has loaned you to your parents, they are responsible to you, and they love you.

You have to obey the police, your boss, the umpire, your teacher—whether you want to or not, whether they like you or not.

It's strange that it's easier to disobey your parents than the boss or the cops. The boss can say, "Do it or you're fired." The cop can tell you, "Shape up or you'll go to jail." Your parents won't say anything like that. They will stick by you, even when you disobey.

The sad thing is, they suffer. The boss and the police officer won't lose much sleep if you disobey. But your parents care. Your disobedience really hurts them.

Your parents may make mistakes. They don't have all wisdom. But they tell you what to do or not to do according to what they believe is best for you. And most likely, with their longer experience, they have more wisdom than you.

Suppose no one had to obey anyone? Suppose all of us did just what we wanted to do? You wouldn't like that kind of world.

The only time you are not to obey your parents is if they order you to do something wrong. But no mother would teach her daughter to steal a car. No father would ask his son to sell heroin. Young people may think that their parents are stupid or behind the times, and that it's silly to do what they command. But it may just be that it's the son or daughter who is stupid and silly.

When Absalom rebelled against his father, David, he broke his father's heart. When the prodigal son left home, his father never stopped longing for him to come back.

Your parents care, and God promises blessings when you obey them.

FINDING EXCUSES

Most of us are good at finding excuses for things we don't want to do. We're not alone. Moses tried excuses too.

One day Moses was startled by a voice coming out of a burning bush. It was God, telling him to return to Egypt and lead the people of Israel to the promised land.

Moses found excuses. "I'm not important enough to make any impression on the Pharaoh," he said. "The Israelites will not believe me or listen to me. I'm no speaker, and a leader has to be a speaker." Finally he pleaded, "Send someone else." Then God lost patience: "the anger of the Lord was kindled against Moses" (Exod. 4:14). So Moses gave in and went.

After a series of plagues, Pharaoh let the Israelites go. During the 40 years in the wilderness, Moses was at times ready to give up. He cried to God, "What shall I do with this people? They are almost ready to stone me" (Exod 17:4).

In spite of all his excuses, Moses did obey. He did lead the people out of Egypt, he did rule them 40 years in the wilderness, and, from the top of Mt. Nebo, before he died at the age of 120, he did glimpse the promised land.

When you know you ought to do something that's right and you don't want to, think of Moses. You too will probably say, "I'm not very important, so what does it matter what I do?" Or, "I simply don't have what it takes." Or, "People will misunderstand, and I'll get into trouble." Or simply, "I don't want to do it." None of these excuses worked for Moses. God didn't let him off.

The fact is, God never lets us off from doing what's right. We may get into trouble. That's OK with God. He knows we're sorry, and he'll forgive us. But if we try to cover up, he won't buy our excuses, because he has promised to help with his own power, as he helped Moses. When we do what's right, we're on God's side and he's on ours. He'll see us through.

THE GOD WHO FORGETS

"They shall all know me, from the least of them to the greatest, says the Lord; for I will forgive their iniquity, and I will remember their sin no more" (Jer. 31:34).

As a young man, St. Augustine lived a self-centered and sinful life. When he turned to the Lord for forgiveness and began a new life of obedience, he wished he could forget the sins of his youth, but he couldn't. God could forget, and he did.

Let's imagine that you die, and suddenly you come face to face with God. You tremble, wondering what's going to happen now. God says nothing, and you break the silence.

"I'm sorry, God, for the times I disobeyed and made my parents unhappy."

"Did you? I don't seem to have any record of that."

"But, God, you must remember the time I drank some beer and smashed the car against a bridge. I spent the night in jail."

"Sorry, I must have forgotten."

"How about all those years when I hardly ever prayed or went to church? I didn't love you."

God pages in his big book and says, "The record must be blotted out. I see nothing."

You see, God does forget. If we're sorry and come to Jesus for forgiveness, he blots out all our transgressions. That's hard to believe. But Jesus has taken our sins upon himself. He does away with our sins, as far as the east is from the west.

He wants us to forget too, but, like Augustine, we may not be able. The people we wronged who have forgiven us would like to forget too, but the memory of the wrong keeps bobbing up now and then.

You'll have to live with a touch of sadness all your life, when you remember how you fail. But your sadness is mixed with a great gladness. God both forgives and forgets. With him, you're OK. You can walk up to him boldly, as if you never once did wrong in your whole life.

HOW GOD HONORS YOU

Whether you like it or not, God's way of honoring you is to give you problems.

Some problems are created by human need and imagination, others by sin and neglect.

Orville and Wilbur Wright started with a problem: how can people fly? Almost every invention or discovery grew out of a problem. God puts a problem in the lap of someone who says, "It's never been done, but I think it can be." The remarkable thing about people is their ability to do something for the first time.

The world is faced with some age-old problems, like war, hunger, poverty, injustice. It also has some relatively new problems, like pollution, overpopulation, the atom bomb. They're all big problems. You might want to give up on them before you start. But we know the names of people like Jane Addams and George Washington Carver because they worked to solve these big problems. You can too.

You may also have problems near at hand. Things are a bit messed up in your home or school. Or maybe you feel like you yourself are the problem. You're about fed up, ready to quit.

Remember that God puts problems in your hands as a way of honoring you. Don't ever tell God to let you off. Don't ever ask him to give you a life without problems. If you had no problems, you might as well be in heaven right now. God gives you problems, and he also helps you solve them.

You may have another 50 or more years to live. Wouldn't it be wonderful if you could help solve the massive problems of war and hunger and poverty? Already scientists and people in government, in your country and in other lands, are hard at work on these very problems. You can be on their team.

Don't sit around and say it can't be done. Ask God to show you how. He has promised to show you and to be on hand whenever you make a good try.

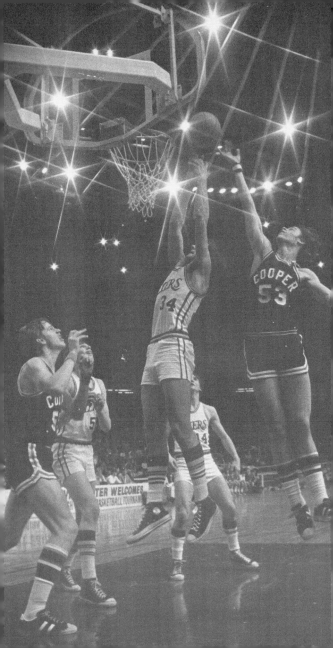

WHO KEEPS YOUR SCORE?

You have all sorts of scorekeepers. Your teacher is one. He or she puts a grade in the record book for you.

Your boss is another. He or she decides whether you're doing your job well or not.

Sometimes you let your friends keep score. You let them decide whether you're OK or not. If their rules go against God's rules, you should not pay any attention to the score they give you.

If you get into the habit of always letting someone else keep your score, you sell your soul to others, to the world.

If that's happened, and you are later elected to government, for instance, you'll always be doing what other people want you to do, instead of what you know you should do.

Often, when the world scores someone as a "success," it means that he or she has become rich, no matter how, or powerful, no matter how. He or she may have lied, cheated, and crushed friends to get a good score.

That's not how Jesus scores. When a person charges unreasonable fees and gets rich, Jesus probably puts a big, fat zero in the records.

It's not easy to ignore phony scorers. If you help other people when you could be helping yourself, the scorers will say you're stupid. If you lose an election or a sale because you're honest, they'll score you as not very bright.

Instead of trying to please them, let Jesus set the rules of the game, and then keep your own score. You may not score yourself very high against the high standards of Jesus. But you'll be playing by the right rules.

Even people who play by the wrong rules know deep down that you are playing the only game that brings long-range satisfaction and joy. You have integrity and character.

Jesus will be pleased. He'll forgive when you fall short, and help you do better next time.

ON JUDGING
OTHERS

If you're the umpire in a ball game, you have to judge whether a player is safe or out. If you're a teacher, you have to judge whether a student should get a *B* or an *A*. If you're the judge in a court of law, you have to weigh evidence and decide if a person is guilty or not guilty.

But Jesus said, "Judge not, that you be not judged." What did he mean? He meant we are not to decide who is a Christian and who is not. He alone knows.

One of the saddest things that happens in a church, or in a family, is someone deciding he can tell who belongs to the Lord and who doesn't.

If you do that, you're trying to be God. It's God's business alone to judge what's in the heart of a person. Your only concern must be that he finds you faithful in your heart. You can't even judge your own heart for sure, and must pray that you be forgiven for perhaps deceiving yourself.

You are a Christian because you trust in Jesus for your salvation. You can't decide who else has that trust in his heart. Only God knows that.

People are different. Suppose two people fall in love. One tells everybody how wonderful his beloved sweetheart is. The other tells no one. He hardly dares tell the one he loves. You can't say that the noisiest one loves the most.

The person who talks most about Jesus may not be the one who loves him most. Jesus may know that a quiet person, who doesn't dare get up and give a testimony, may be just the person who would die for the faith.

Jesus said that love is the test. If you start this business of judging others, you'll probably end up not loving those you judge, and not wanting to be with them. Then you're in deep trouble with Jesus.

Thank God that his family is big enough for many kinds of Christians, big enough even for you.

WHEN YOU'RE LONELY

If you're lonely, you're no different from others. Everybody is lonely sometime. It's even a good thing to be lonely, because it shows you need the love of other people.

If you should be so selfish that you didn't care whether people liked you or not, then you'd be in a bad way.

But to be lonely all of the time, or most of the time, is not good.

One thing is sure; if you're lonely, it won't help to go to the bus station where lots of people are milling around. They're probably all strangers, and they couldn't care less about you.

One way to stop being lonely is to think of the people who do care for you. Even if they're a hundred miles away, just remembering they care will make you less lonely.

If you have trouble thinking of anyone who really cares for you, then start thinking of people you ought to care for. That will put you on the right track.

Do you remember Jesus' story of the good Samaritan? Do you think the Samaritan was lonely very often? He most likely traveled alone, and he probably wasn't even looking for friends. But he had his eye out for someone who might need a friend. And he found a beaten man in the ditch to help.

All of us are little worlds of our own. Like planets spinning in space, each of us is separate from every other person. You might have a close friend, but a friend cannot altogether enter your world, nor can you enter your friend's. There will be some loneliness in every life.

We sing "What a Friend We Have in Jesus." We know Jesus has promised always to be there, waiting for us to let him be our friend. He is lonely for us, and deep down we're lonely for him.

If you let him come, he'll bring with him some lonely person who needs you as a friend. And Jesus says, "Go to him. By being his friend, you'll be my friend too."

FEELING SORRY FOR YOURSELF

"**I** complained that I had no shoes, until I met a man who had no feet."

To feel sorry for yourself is bad business. Let someone else feel sorry for you, if they want to, but don't you. The moment you do, you'll turn people away. Self-pity is a kind of social leprosy. Who wants to be with someone who's moping and sulking?

It's an easy thing to do. Someone has more money or clothes than you. Someone makes the team, and you don't. Someone takes trips, and you stay home. Someone gets better grades in school.

Maybe you're looking the wrong direction. Someone is blind, and you see. Someone has a damaged brain, but you can think. Half the world is hungry; you can eat. Someone is dying from leukemia; you are well. You could have been born in a primitive jungle; you live in a world of convenience and opportunity.

Helen Keller was both blind and deaf. For years she was imprisoned in darkness and silence. Then a skilled and loving teacher came into her life, and with almost miraculous patience opened up the world for her through touch. Helen Keller became a warm, cheerful, and inspiring person.

Feeling sorry for yourself is a kind of disease. Even if you get everything you think you want, you might very well keep on wanting something else, and still feel sorry.

The best cure is to start listing all the good things God has promised and already delivered to you. It will be a long list. His withholding of things you want may be good too. People who seem to have everything are often miserable. They get fed up with things they have, and sit around feeling sorry for themselves.

Shake the mood. Get off that old horse of self-pity. He'll get you nowhere.

YOU'RE NOT A CAMERA

You take a picture of your friend. Even with the best lens, you can't photograph your friend's loves or fears or hates. The camera sees only so much, and no more.

God has promised to let you see far more than any photograph lets you see. With the lens of faith, you can see beyond the best microscope or telescope.

You see that behind this vast universe is the Creator God, who is your Father. You see that Jesus, the carpenter, is your Savior and your Lord.

You may have friends who think God and Jesus and heaven are not real. That's too bad for them. They live in a flat world, like the world a worm sees. You soar like an eagle, with a gleam of eternity in your eye.

Most important, you see God as a God of love. That's not always easy. When things go wrong, when your plans fall apart, and when even your prayers seem to go unanswered, you may wonder where God is hiding.

But with the eye of faith, you see beyond the cloud of disappointment. You know God has not forgotten you. He has promised never to leave you. If some doors seem to close, he's working to open others and to guide you to them.

Remember the story of Job in the Old Testament? A rich and honored man, he lost his property, his children—everything—and finally he was down with a terrible disease. In this horrible condition, he still cried, "I know that my Redeemer lives, and at last he will stand upon the earth. . . . I shall see God."

With only the eyes of a camera, Job would have been crushed by his troubles. But beyond the wreckage, he saw a God who loved him.

This is the faith God has promised us.

THE COMPANY YOU KEEP

The church is the greatest company on earth, and you belong to it through Baptism.

The church is broken up into three large parts: the Roman Catholic Church, the Eastern or Orthodox Church, and the Protestant Church. Of course, there are millions of congregations. But they all have the same Lord, so they form one church.

When the Lord promised to send the Holy Spirit, who would have dreamed so many people would now be Christians? Probably about 100 people huddled together in the upper room that first Pentecost. They heard a wind, and they saw tongues of fire on the heads of their friends.

Something strange and powerful was happening. The church was born. A colony of heaven was planted on earth. The landing on the moon was as nothing compared with this. You are of this colony.

If you're in some bleachers with 100,000 people at a football game, that's small stuff compared with the company you join as you sit in church. If all the company were to be together in one place, they would fill a stadium seating about a billion people. When you sit in church on Sunday morning, imagine you are a section of this vast stadium.

If a tremendous explosion were to blow the whole world into bits, the people in this stadium would simply be transported to another, greater stadium in the empire over which our Lord rules. Without any explosion, when you die, the Lord will put you on your feet again in that kingdom. After all, you are eternal. You are ticketed to live with him forever.

Be proud and very thankful that God promised you can belong to his company. Never apologize for being a Christian. It is the greatest thing about you.

NO BUSY
SIGNAL

God's line is never busy. You'd think someone who manages the whole universe would take some time off. But he doesn't. It's almost as if he sits waiting for your call.

And he listens. The whole world is full of poor listeners. But not God. He has promised to hear you out, anytime.

He understands the hundreds of languages of earth. He even understands you when you don't use words at all. Sometimes you have a hard time putting into words what you want to say. Perhaps you only cry, "God, help me." He reads your mind and heart, and knows what you want to tell him, even when you don't quite know yourself.

Or you may use words other people have written for you, like the Lord's Prayer. Some of these prayers say more than you could think of saying. That's good. They become your words, your prayer.

It may be a good thing not to leave praying to chance, but to have fixed times to dial him, like the first thing in the morning, or at meals, or the last thing before you fall asleep.

Of course, you can pray walking down the street, or sitting at your desk, or riding down the highway. Anytime, anywhere is a good time and place to talk with God.

You may get together with others and have a cluster for prayer—especially in the church service, where everyone has come specifically to pray and to praise. You would not want to miss this weekly appointment to thank God.

The wonderful thing about God is that he hears more than you can possibly put into words. He hears the fears and hopes and disappointments that you may be hiding from everyone else.

He will sort out your prayers and give you what is good. He knows what that is much better than anyone else.

GO AHEAD,
BE ANGRY

Be angry, then, but not at God!

When you sulk or cheat or loaf around and get nothing done, go ahead, be disgusted with yourself.

Go ahead, be mad at a world that lets wars kill, that gets people hung up on drugs and alcohol, that lets gangsters murder, that lets millions go hungry while other millions die from overeating.

You can find all sorts of situations in the world to make your blood boil. And that's good, if you don't just sit around and fret and blame everyone else, if you try to do something about it. After all, God is angry too at this state of affairs, and you join him in being furious about things that rob people of love and joy.

As a young man, Abraham Lincoln saw black people whipped and sold like cattle, and he was enraged. When he finally had the chance, he issued the Emancipation Proclamation and set them free.

Love and anger are like two sides of the same coin. If a pusher is selling dope to your best friend, you won't just wring your hands and wish it weren't happening. You'll be mad enough to do something.

You can be angry and sad at the same time. If things are not happy in your home, or at school or in church don't be too quick to blame someone. Without fixing the blame on your parents or the teacher or the pastor, perhaps you can do something to make things better. It's amazing what God can do through one person who gets stirred up enough to use love and patience to change things. Even great world problems can be solved by someone who is concerned and angry enough to become God's agent.

Indignation against wrong makes you God's partner.

CAN YOU HURT JESUS?

Jesus rose from the dead, ascended to heaven, and is seated at the right hand of the Father, in power. He had his time of suffering and death. You can't hurt Jesus anymore, can you?

You know you can!

He died to save you, to forgive your sins, and to make a place for you with him in his Father's house forever. He is your everlasting friend.

You can forget all about him, and you often do. And that hurts.

You can live a life of selfishness and fear and worry, as if Jesus is not around, and that hurts.

You can doubt that he either can or will do anything for you, and that hurts.

You can give up on yourself, and say that nothing matters anymore. Remember whose salvation he was buying when he paid that big price on the cross. If you think you're nothing, that hurts him.

When you treat someone like dirt, or when someone needs you and you do nothing, it's as if you did this to Jesus. That's what he said, remember?

He loves you, that's why you can hurt him. The people you love most are the people who can hurt you the most and whom you can hurt the most. If you want to keep from getting hurt, don't love anyone.

But Jesus didn't play it safe. He risked loving you and everyone else. He opened himself up for sorrow and pain. And he can't turn it off. He loves and loves for all time, forever. So the cross was not the end of his suffering.

You need not only hurt him. You can make his heart glad too. When you're sorry and come to him for forgiveness, he's glad. When you do what he wants you to do, he's glad.

Sometimes you will hurt him, because you will fail him. But you can also make him glad.

AM I SO DIFFERENT?

"**H**e's different, you know." Would you like someone to say that about you?

It all depends on what they mean, of course. If they mean you're stupid, or crippled, or nasty-tempered, then it hurts.

But if they mean you just don't fit in with the gang, that's another matter. Perhaps no really decent person should fit in.

Let's ask, "What's so bad about being different?" God made everyone different from everyone else. If you're always trying to be like someone else, you're in trouble. To say, "I'd sure like to be smart like her, or rich like him, or pretty like her"—that's committing the sin of envy, one of the seven deadly sins. God says, "Stop envying others. Do your best with what I've given you."

President Roosevelt was "different." He suffered polio at the age of 39. But he didn't throw in the sponge. He's the only four-term president the United States has had, and he couldn't walk a step.

Don't ever wish you were someone else. When you envy others, you probably end up not liking them. And you end up not liking yourself. Someone said envy has the ugliness of a trapped rat gnawing its own foot in its effort to escape.

Besides, you really don't know the feelings and troubles another person might have. If you knew, you might never want to exchange with that person.

The *you* God made is a good you. You're different, and be thankful you are. If you're a piccolo, don't wish you were a tuba or violin or French horn. A piccolo, well played, can produce beautiful music.

You're not an accident, remember. You are you because God let you be born. And God is not partial to one child over another. He thinks you're great. You should too.

SOMEONE NEEDS YOU

You are needed. Otherwise God would not have let you be born, nor would he keep you around.

Sometimes that's hard to believe. When you're down, you might say, "If I died, who would care? The world would get along without me." But God doesn't want the world to get along without you.

Your family needs you. You might think they'd be relieved if you ran away. That's not true. There'd be great sadness in their hearts if you were to disappear. They probably need you more than you need them.

Someone who is lonely needs you. There are many people who would be much happier if you became their friend.

Some job needs you. You may not know what kind. But God has given you abilities and qualities that fit beautifully into some work waiting for you. He expects you to develop those abilities and get ready.

Your church needs you. Some very ordinary things, like choir, Sunday school, youth groups, could use you. Even just being there every Sunday is important. Someone will say it was good to see you in church. People want you and need you. And, of course, to say a good word for the Lord and the church whenever you have a chance—the Lord himself needs you for that.

Suppose Abraham Lincoln, as a boy in a log cabin in Indiana, had said, "Who can ever need me? My father is poor, I'm awkward, I can hardly read." Or suppose Joan of Arc, savior of France, had said, "I'm only a peasant girl. What's life got for me?" Or suppose Booker T. Washington, founder of Tuskegee Institute, had said, "I'm black, the son of a slave. How can I be needed?"

You're probably not another Lincoln, but don't sell yourself short. You are needed, today and tomorrow. God will show you where.

WHEN PEOPLE PRAISE YOU

Be on your guard. You may begin to think you're really somebody, better than others. And you'll end up being stuck-up and proud, with no one liking you.

You don't need to. You can be thankful for praise and still be liked. But you'll have to remember some things.

Remember that everything you are and have comes from God. It's not yours to keep. You have it only as a loan, to use. Your brain, the air you breathe, the ground you walk on, your country, your school, your opportunities, your very life—they're all gifts from God. And you can't really be proud of a gift. You can be pleased and thankful, but not proud.

Remember how Jesus handled praise. He kept reminding people that he could do nothing at all unless the Father gave him the power to do it. If Jesus had broken the world's marathon record, he would have said, "My Father in heaven gave me the skill and power to run the race."

If you are a football star, or a good pianist, or an A student, and people praise you, can you remember that you'd have none of these abilities unless God had loaned them to you? Remember, too, that you could get a brain tumor, or have an accident, and your abilities would be gone.

Some people have the habit of praising you just to make you feel good, whether you deserve it or not. Some people may even be counting on getting you to do something for them.

Most people who praise you really mean it, and it's nice to hear good things said about you. Even the Bible encourages this. But it also warns us to be on our toes not to think more highly of ourselves than we should.

Be glad God has given you the kind of abilities good people like to see, and praise him for his gifts.

HOW RELIGIOUS ARE YOU?

Maybe you don't feel religious at all. What if going to church and reading the Bible bore you?

What if zooming along on a motorcycle or flying down a hill on skis makes you happier than thinking about God?

What if you have a hard time hoping for the future or loving other people? What if doubts of all kinds keep pushing in?

OK, you don't feel very religious at all. Does that mean you're not a follower of Jesus, that you're not a Christian?

Not necessarily. Jesus never promised you one kind of feeling or another. He didn't command you to feel religious. He knows you don't always have control of your feelings. Sometimes you're up, sometimes down.

Jesus came down hard on what you do, not on how you feel. He said whoever *does* the will of his Father is my disciple.

For instance, you don't like a certain person who's lonely and discouraged. Because

Jesus told you to love your neighbor, you set out to be the person's friend, even if you don't feel like it at all. You may almost feel like a phony, pretending to like the person. But something strange is likely to happen. If you do kind things for a person, you'll probably begin to like him or her.

What about going to church? You know Christ wants you there, so you go. You pray. You thank him for dying for you and for giving you good things. You listen carefully to the preaching, to see if God has some word for you in the sermon. And who knows, the Spirit of God may bless you with joy you never thought possible.

Don't ask yourself, "How religious do I feel?" Ask rather, "How am I doing, Lord?" And he may say, "You're coming along. Keep going."

God will give you feelings of trust and hope and deep satisfaction when you least expect it.

YOUR MANY CIRCLES

 think of your life in six circles, six kinds of people you live with.

In the first circle (a big one) are many, many people you'll never know. You don't know the people who make the shoes you wear, who produce the food you eat, or who manufacture the bike you ride. You don't know who they are, but you depend on them.

Then there's a large circle of all the people you simply know. You don't go camping with them or invite them to your home. You just know them, that's all.

In the next circle, a smaller one, are your friends. Some are very close friends. You spend time together. You write to each other. You may be friends for life.

Then there's the circle of your family— your parents, brothers, sisters, aunts, uncles, even cousins. You were born, or adopted, into this circle. You belong to them, and they belong to you.

The time may come when you love someone so much (and in a different way from anyone else) that the two of you will become a new family, husband and wife. This is the smallest, tightest, and most wonderful human circle of all. In this circle you give yourself to each other in a sexual life which may be the beginning of another family.

Preparing yourself for this wonderful circle is one of the most important things you do. To give your sex life to others is to risk having this small circle be less wonderful than it can be.

There is still another circle, different from the others. It is made up of you and Christ and all others who have been drawn into Christ. This circle is different, because it doesn't end with death. You are Christ's forever. When you die, in this group (called the holy Christian church) you simply get transferred to heaven. This is the most lasting circle of all.

Thank God for all the circles.

LOVE
AND SEX

The sex act and a love that lasts belong together. If you separate them, you get hurt, others get hurt, and you disobey God.

In a different way, hunger and food also belong together. You eat to satisfy your hunger.

Wanting sex is much different from wanting food. It takes one person to eat. It takes two to have sex. You don't fall in love with ice cream, and your heart isn't broken if the restaurant runs out of hamburger.

You may think you can use someone for sex and then go on, unhurt and satisfied, like after eating a hamburger. But you can't. You'll know you cheated on something very wonderful and beautiful. You have said yes to sex, but no to a great and lasting love.

God expects a couple to want more than sex from each other. Both must want a lasting love, as in marriage. If one of you wants to love "till death do us part," and the other turns away, there will be deep hurt. If both

want nothing to do with this lifelong love, and if they use sex much as they eat when they're hungry, then they make the great gift of sex into something coarse and ugly.

Many people will tell you that this high and cherished notion of sex is old-fashioned and rather silly, and that no one thinks like that anymore. People have said that for centuries, and they've been wrong. All sorts of people have discovered how wrong they were, sometimes too late to enter the world of great love.

Jesus has promised to forgive all our sins. But sin leaves wounds. And wounds, even if healed, leave scars. This is true of the sins of sex as well as the sins of hatred, theft, and murder. Scars are memories, and sometimes they keep hurting a long time.

God hopes we don't have to be hurt. If we try to obey him in all we do, we will have a minimum amount of hurt.

YOUR OWN RULES

Christ gave us one big rule: You shall love the Lord your God with all your heart, and with all your soul, and with all your mind, and your neighbor as yourself.

People make rules for themselves, sometimes called self-disciplines. Here are some samples:

I read at least one book a week.

At nine o'clock each morning I say a prayer for my country and for the president.

I go to church, some church, wherever I happen to be, every Sunday.

I do 50 push-ups each day.

I give one-tenth of my earnings to the church.

I limit myself to watching 30 minutes of TV each day.

I write at least one letter each week.

I memorize one new verse of the Bible each week.

I find some place to be by myself to meditate 15 minutes each day.

I have a written list of people I pray for each day.

These are not rules God has laid down, but he may like many, perhaps all, of them.

Try having some rules of your own. They keep you from drifting along without direction. Some of this list may appeal to you. You may think up even better ones.

Oliver Wendell Holmes, Supreme Court justice, said he went to church every Sunday without fail, because a little plant in his heart needed watering once a week.

Most of us don't like to have others impose their rules on us. It's different when we make our own rules. We put ourselves under discipline. And that's good.

Most people of strength have their own rules to follow. These rules become habits. Good habits help you do good things with less and less effort.

God's one rule of love is the big one. But within that big rule, you can have many little rules of your own to help you obey God's big one.

THE GREAT SUPPER

If an angel should come to your door with a letter for you, you'd probably be scared. But you would open the letter. Suppose it said:

I am coming to your town and I invite you to have supper with me.

(signed) Jesus Christ

Would you go, or would you throw the invitation aside and forget it? Of course you would go.

Jesus *has* prepared a supper, and the invitation is for you. You won't see him at the table, but he has promised to be there, in bread and wine—his body and his blood.

If you forget to go, it might be for several reasons. Maybe you don't really believe he is there, or you don't especially care to be with him. Or maybe you can't believe the invitation is really for you.

It's a pity, even a tragedy, if you fail to show up, because this meal has in it the very things your soul needs. Without those things, your soul becomes so undernourished that it dies.

This meal has the forgiveness of sins. Jesus gave his body and shed his blood to wipe out all your guilt and sin.

The meal has new joy and fellowship. We are drawn into Christ, and we are drawn to one another. It is a family supper.

The meal has love. The first of these suppers was on the night before Jesus was crucified. He loved these disciples, as he loves us, and he wanted them, and us, never to forget how much he loves us.

You may not feel great excitement when you come to the Lord's Supper. But you must believe that it's all there—the Lord and all his gifts—and that having feasted with him, you leave with blessings too wonderful to know or feel.

Next time you come to Holy Communion, thank the Lord for inviting you, thank him for nourishing your life with his gifts, and thank him for letting you be in his great family.

SAY YES TO THE FUTURE

The future is in God's hands. That's why you can say *yes*.

Some people look into the future, and all they see is a dark cave filled with poisonous snakes and deep pits. They inch their way, every step filled with fear.

That's too bad. The future is not a dark cave with snakes lurking. It's a beautiful rolling land, and your Father is there.

As you approach the shining palace in the distance, your final home, you do run into enemies—disease, war, crime, and suffering. And death will be the last enemy. But your Father is there to fight for you, and to pick you up when you get hurt. And when death is through with you, your Father ushers you through the last, great door into the blazing light of his castle—your home forever.

Keep your eye on the palace and your Father during these swift years you have on earth. Remember that on the way nothing can separate you from the love of God.

How do you suppose you have made it so far? Didn't God let you be born? Hasn't he given you parents, friends, a country, a body, a brain, food on your table? Hasn't he died for you? Can you for one minute think he would let you down?

You haven't lived too many years, but they are enough for you to know God has had his hand in yours. You are very dear to him.

You cannot know what lies ahead. Maybe the future will be much better than anything in the past. It could also plunge you into periods of suffering and testing.

But it's your Father's world, and you are your Father's child. His hand will be in yours all the way. So say *yes* to the future.

For you there will really be no end. On the other side of death, Jesus waits to fulfill his promise, "In my Father's house are many rooms . . . ; I go to prepare a place for you. . . . I will come again and will take you to myself, that where I am you may be also" (John 14:2-3).

FORGIVE ME
THE PROMISE
I BROKE

I meant to keep it, Lord. I didn't plan to break it.

I'm not sure what happened. I guess I forgot both you and promises.

I won't blame anyone but myself. Sure, the crowd helped me forget. But I was the one who lost my head. I was the stupid one.

I hadn't been praying much. And I had lost touch with the church and my friends there. It's easy to forget when you don't pray and when you're with people who don't care.

You understand, God, don't you, that I like to be wanted? It's hard to be on the outside.

I realize now that you don't do everything others want you to do, just to be wanted and to be on the inside. The price gets to be too high—especially when I break promises I've made to you.

I'm glad you won't turn me out. I count on your promise to forgive, and to let me make another try. Amen.

I WASN'T FAIR, LORD

Forgive me, Lord, for making promises I never intended to keep. You knew, of course. I can't fool you.

But it wasn't fair. It was a dishonest thing to do. The people who heard me make the promises, like the pastor and the congregation, didn't know. They were glad to hear me say the words.

But you knew, and I knew.

Now I want to make a fresh start. I make the promises over again—to you. I really do want to be your child. I really want to turn away from everything that's wrong. I really want to believe in you and do your will.

I'm miserable every time I think of the cheap trick I tried to play. From now on, I promise to pray and to take church seriously. I want you near me, to help me.

I'll probably do some stumbling, and you'll have to put me on my feet again. But I'll try to be faithful. That's a promise. This time I mean it. Amen.

HELP ME
BE A FRIEND

Is everyone lonely, Lord? Is it hard for us to have friends and to be a friend?

I think I have friends. But would they be my friends if they knew everything about me? Do I dare let them see into my heart? Or do I have to hide the real me from them?

You see everything. You know what I'm like on the inside. And you're still my friend.

Do you think you could make me that kind of friend? I'd like to be like that. I'd like to be a friend to everyone—even to people I don't like. Maybe people I don't like need my friendship most.

I remember your story of the good Samaritan. He was a friend to a stranger. Is that what you want me to be? If I could be that kind of friend, maybe I would never be lonely.

You are my best friend, Lord. Help me be a friend like you. Amen.

I'M COUNTING THEM, LORD

I heard a song about blessings, "Count them, one by one." I decided to do that, Lord, and here's a list.

I know enough to start with the best one, and that's *you*. I may forget sometimes, and think of other things. But I know the greatest gift of all is that you give me yourself.

Then, there is life. If I hadn't been born, I wouldn't have a list at all. And you keep my heart beating. Thanks for life.

And family and friends. What would I do if I didn't have them? You don't really *give* them to me. You *loan* them to me for these years. They love me, and I love them.

I remember that you've given me a country. I may find fault with its government at times, but it's a great country, and I'm glad I belong here.

Then all sorts of other things: eyes to see with and ears to hear with, school, trees, birds, flowers, games—this whole world.

Thanks, Lord!